For David and Mary Wild
E.R. & P.R.

To Ginny and Catherine
for all their help
R.B.C.

SIMON & SCHUSTER BOOKS FOR YOUNG READERS
Simon & Schuster Building, Rockefeller Center
1230 Avenue of the Americas, New York, New York 10020

Published simultaneously in Great Britain by Walker Books Limited.
SIMON & SCHUSTER BOOKS FOR YOUNG READERS
is a trademark of Simon & Schuster.
Manufactured in Hong Kong.
10 9 8 7 6 5 4 3 2 1
Library of Congress Cataloging-in-Publication Data
Rogers, Paul, 1950–   Zoe's tower / by Paul and Emma Rogers ; illustrated
by Robin Bell Corfield.   p.   cm.   Summary: Zoe explores one of her
favorite places before a familiar voice calls her home.
[1. Play—Fiction.]   I. Rogers, Emma.
II. Corfield, Robin Bell, ill.   III. Title.   PZ7.R6257Z0 1991
[E]—dc20   90-48291   CIP   AC
ISBN 0-671-73811-9

ZOE'S TOWER

Story by
Paul and Emma Rogers

Watercolors by
Robin Bell Corfield

SIMON & SCHUSTER BOOKS FOR YOUNG READERS

Published by Simon & Schuster
New York • London • Toronto • Sydney • Tokyo • Singapore

If you leave
the warm house
and follow the path,

you come to a leafy lane.

If you go along the lane
and a little bit further,

you come to a wooden gate.

And if you climb over the wooden gate
and march up the muddy track,

you come to a shady wood.

And if you go through the shady wood,
   past where the best blackberries
   hang just out of reach,
   where pheasants flap up startled,

you come to a sunny meadow.

And if you cross the sunny meadow,
   where lapwings go tumbling up into the air,
   where the stream disappears, gurgling,

you come to the place
where Zoe's tower stands.

And if you
climb up
step by step,
past the
scuttling spider,
past the slit where
the wind whistles,
past the ledge with
the empty nest,

you come out under the sky
where the crows wheel and dive.

And if you stand on tiptoe,

you can see the whole way that you came...

and a little bit further.

And if you listen,
in the wind you can hear
someone calling,

And then
you know

that it's time
to go…

home.